UNBELIEVABLE BOOK OF POETRY

BY ERIKA ROTH

© 2004
FUZZY MIND PUBLICATIONS
NEW PORT RICHEY, FL

REPRINTED BY PERMISSION
GRIDLEY FIRES BOOKS – 2018

ISBN: 978-1-64255-887-6

DEDICATION

I dedicate this book to my imagination
and of course
my teacher and her support
in my writing

TABLE OF CONTENTS

Color Poem

Blue is the surrounding sky around the sun
and water that drips from the faucet and an
ice cold, berry blue slushie, that melts in
the heat. Blue is the taste of cotton candy
that dissolves in my mouth. Steamy hot pie
that just came out of the oven and squishy
bubble gum, smell blue. Rain that drops from
my roof after a storm, makes me feel blue.

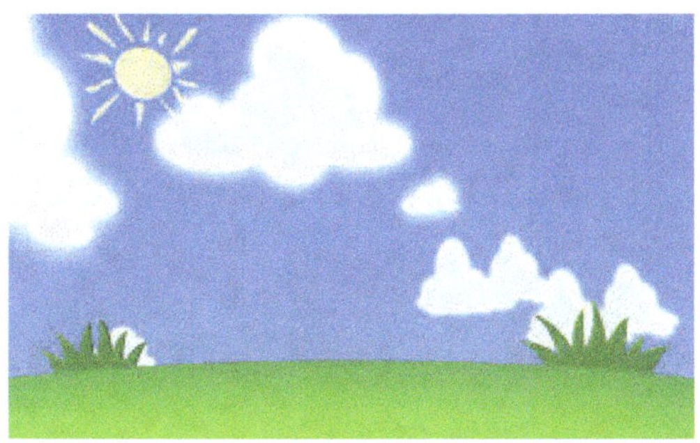

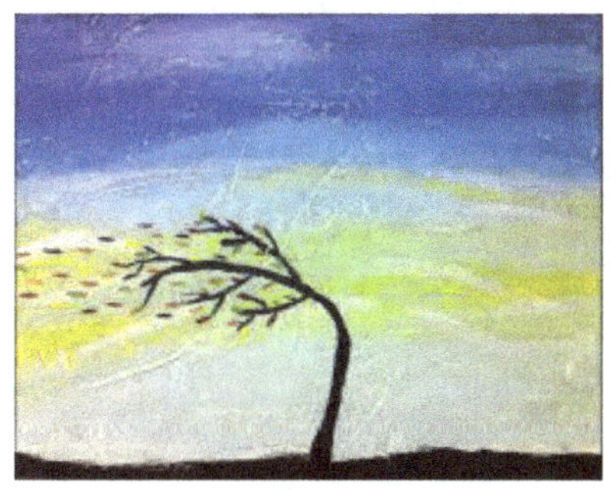

Haiku

Trees sway in the wind
    animals are scurrying
        twister is coming

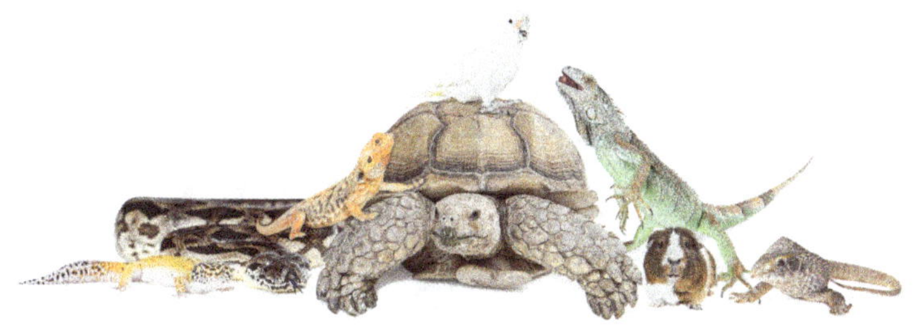

Diamanté

Reptiles
scaly   effective
hiding peering glaring
water land survival teeth
hunting biting creeping
speedy determined
mammals

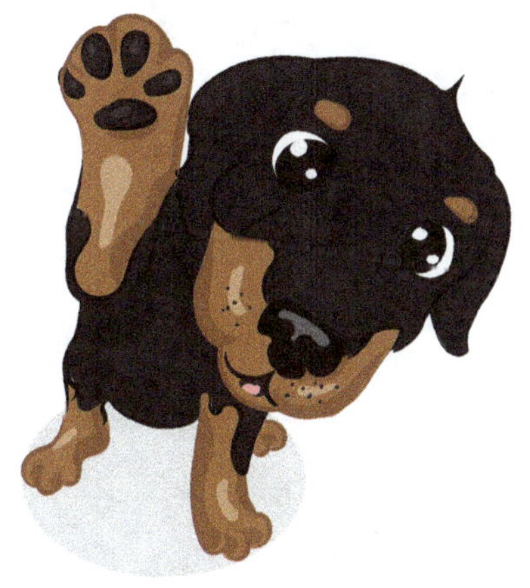

Formula

Dog
Rottweiler slobbering
Stubborn playful
hyperactive

Limerick

Miss Goodell
she tripped and fell
she got hurt
landed in the dirt
WOW! She's suddenly well!

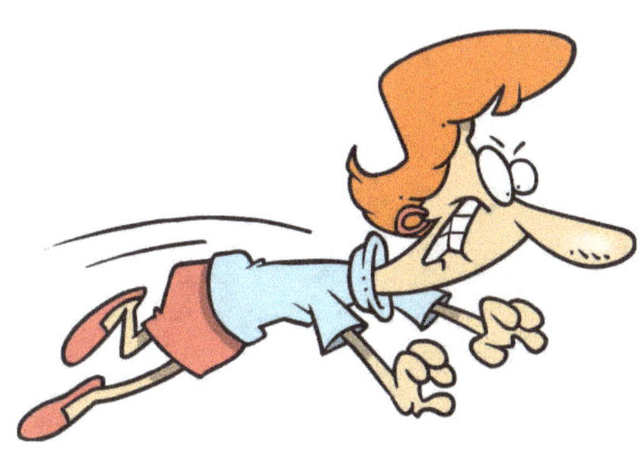

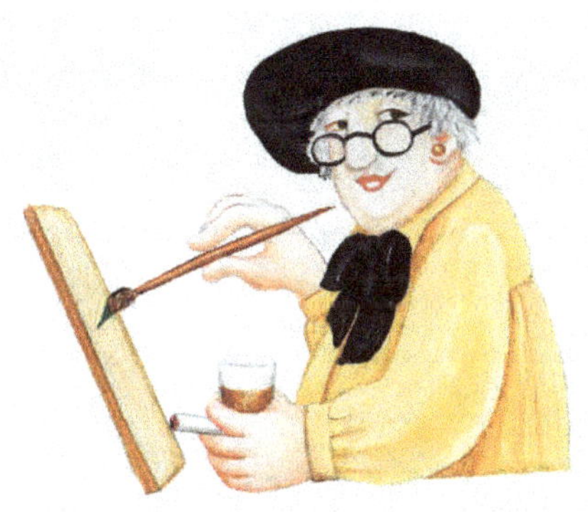

Clerihew

The Artist

There once was an artist
She was the largest,
but people loved her for her work,
And her breaking record of a burp!

I Am

Me

I am a non-believer in animal experiments
and I am a hard worker.
I wonder what the first living thing on earth was.
I see black shadows.
I want my parents to get back together.
I am a non-believer in animal experiments
and I am a hard worker.
I pretend normal items are spy gadgets.
I feel excited when I come across a lion.
I touch raging water from a crystal blue waterfall.
I worry what my test scores are going to be.
I cry when a loved one dies, including an animal.
I am a non-believer in animal experiments
and I am a hard worker.
I understand what it is like to be grounded.
I dream of a world of magic everywhere!!
I try to do the best I can.
I hope I win the lottery some day.
I am a non-believer in animal experiments
and I am a hard worker.

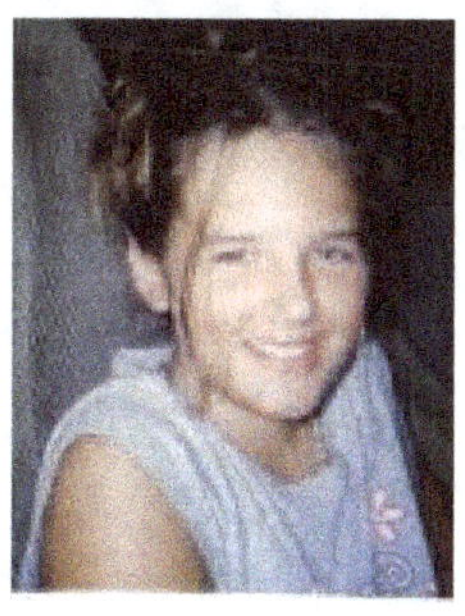

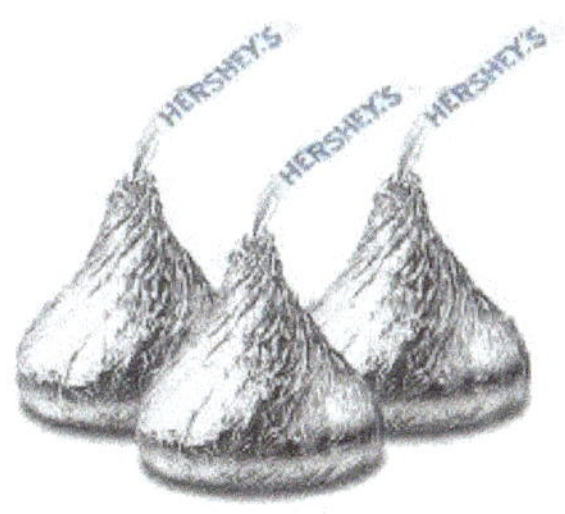

Hershey Kiss

candy,
symmetrical, spectacular
hiding, seeking, laughing,
sweet in a little package!!!!
Hershey's!!!!

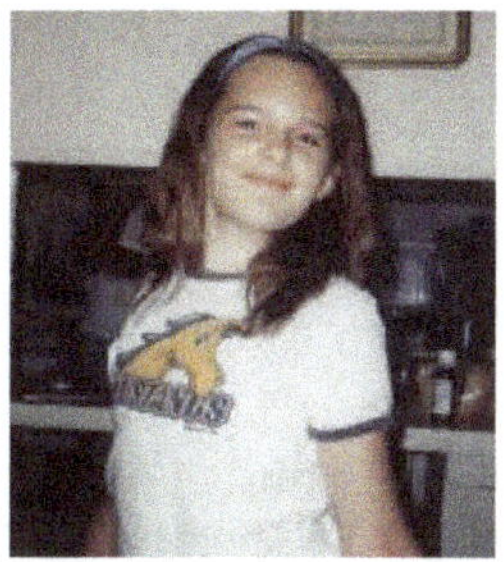

If I Were In Charge Of The World

If I, Erika Roth, were in charge of the world, I'd cancel war,
hatred,
the sale of tobacco products and also
animal experimentation.

If I were in charge of the world,
there'd be lower gas prices,
green grass everywhere and
not so strict teachers, unlike Miss Goodell.

If I were in charge of the world you wouldn't have litter. You
wouldn't have abuse.
You wouldn't have starvation
or "gangs in the alleys."
You wouldn't even have BAD school lunch.

If I were in charge of the world
A homeless child would be a happier person.
All sick people would be cured right away. And a person who
sometimes
forgot to say thank you,
and sometimes forgot to cover their mouth,
Would still be allowed to be in charge of the world.

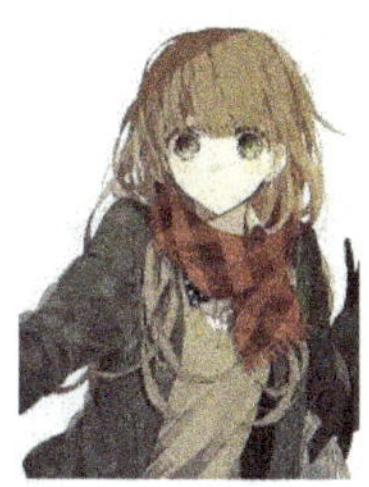

Power Poem

My kingdom is made of candy that only kids could dream of, sour to sweet and flavors you can't beat.

I have long black hair with red on my bangs, and a long blue dress that drags the floor as I walk.

My name is candy, as you can tell, but my friends call me drama queen because I hate bugs!!

I have any power I want, from Ice to to Fire to Weather, and so I have it all!!

I use my powers for good...and revenge...sometimes-
The only rule I have is NO EATING IN THE HOUSE!!
Other than that there are no rules.

I think my followers feel lucky, I mean they do get three meals a day.
I feel spoiled being able to do whatever I want, whenever I want.
I wish that I could ride a shooting star.

Apology

i gave a sarcastic remark
when you told me to clean my room.
i know you are steamed up, because it's happened
more than once.
i'm sorry
plus, the only reason I did it is because,
it's an automatic reaction to be sarcastic.
sweet in a little package!!!!

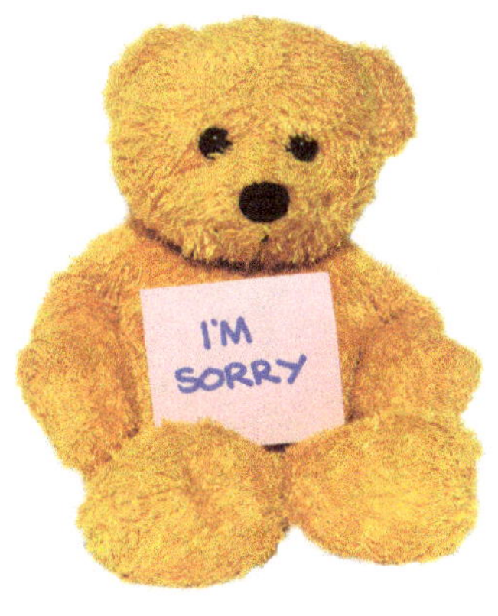

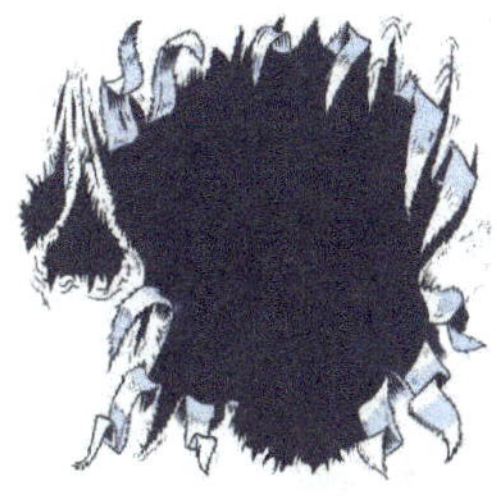

Can You Imagine?

A world without love and care
Or NO lice bugs in your hair

A hose that does not drip
And pants that never rip

A 30 year old without a car
And a child at a bar

A world with no flags
And people walking around wearing rags

An animal that's not tamed
And a person that was never named

Men that did not burp
And nothing to slurp

Everyone had braces
And no shoe laces

It Bugs Me

It bugs me when I stub my toe,
It bugs me when my parents say NO!!

It bugs me when I'm all alone and no-one
Is close to being home.

It bugs me when I'm feeling low,
It bugs me when my friends have to go.

It bugs me when a poem doesn't rhyme
It bugs me when I only have a dime.

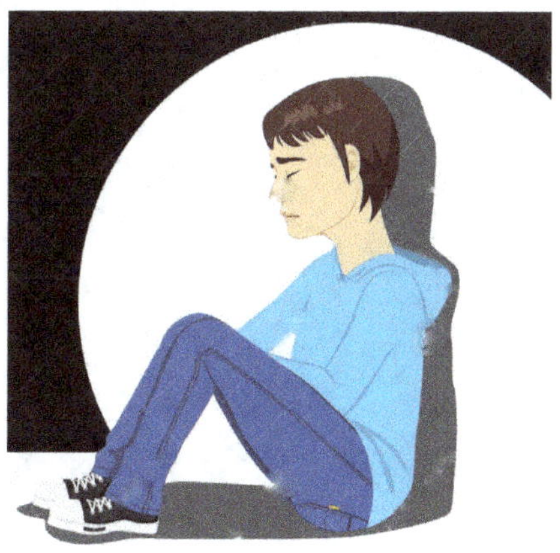

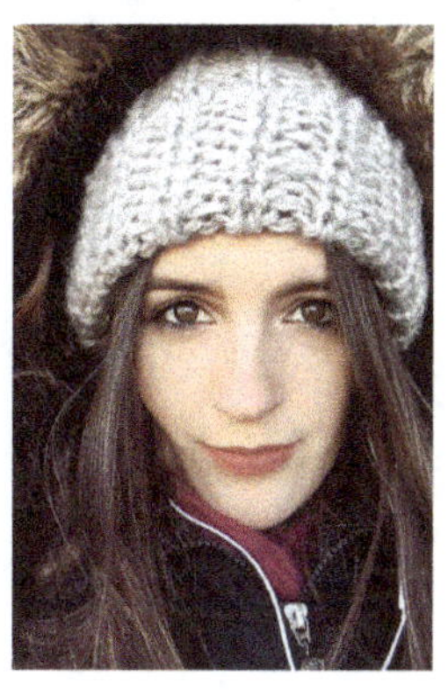

About the Author

Erika Rae Renee (Roth) Owen wrote these
"unbelievable" poems while in the fourth grade.
She's written many more like them
over her student career, along with
numerous stories.
She resides in New York City
with her husband and their kitten, Rummy.